CRAFT HAPPY

Scrapbooking
Your Memories

Craft Happy: Scrapbooking Your Memories
Copyright © 2013 by Editions de Paris Inc.

Published in English in 2013 by:
Harper Design
An Imprint of HarperCollins*Publishers*
10 East 53rd Street
New York, NY 10022
Tel (212) 207-7000
harperdesign@harpercollins.com
www.harpercollins.com

Distributed throughout the world by:
HarperCollins*Publishers*
10 East 53rd Street
New York, NY 10022

This book was originally published in Japanese as
SCRAPAHOLIC BOOK 2.
Japanese edition © 2011 by Editions de Paris Inc.
English translation rights arranged with Editions de Paris Inc.
through ricorico llc.
info@editionsdeparis.com
www.editionsdeparis.com

Crafts creator: Aya Nagaoka
Interior design: Kyoko Matsubayashi, Andrew Pothecary
(forbidden colour)
Photography: Nao Shimizu
Photo archive: Getty Images
Styling: Naoko Horie
Planning and editing: Aya Nagaoka, Miyuki Matsuda
(Editions de Paris)
Special Thanks: Nicky Chung
Translation: Designcraft, Leanne Ogasawara
Chief Editor and Production Manager: Aki Ueda (ricorico)

Library of Congress Control Number: 2013931026

ISBN: 978-0-06224766-7

Printed in China
First printing, 2013

INTRODUCTION

This book was born out of the simple hope that people could enjoy scrapbooking with more freedom, creativity, and lightheartedness. Beginning with several basic techniques, we will continue on with more advanced and sophisticated project ideas. The ideas are offered in a how-to style in the form of thirty projects, which you can use freely and arrange creatively to suit your own style. Scrapbooking is a way to preserve our treasured memories. It can also make our lives richer in the process.

CONTENTS

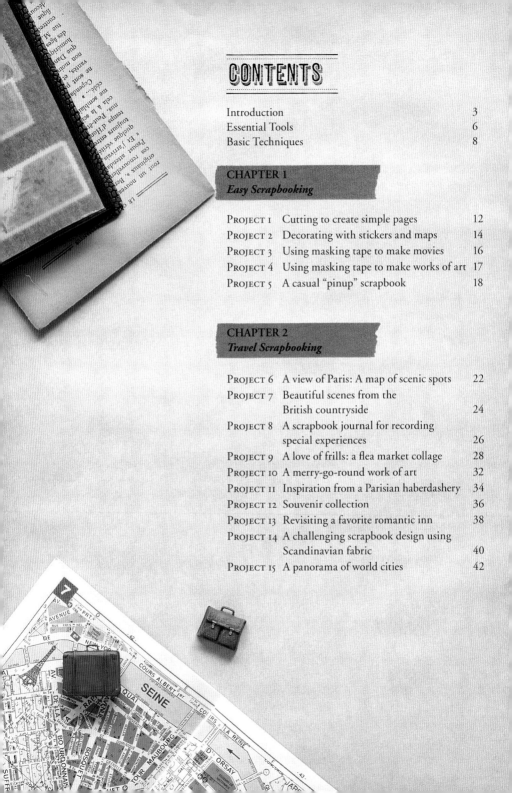

CHAPTER 3
Commemorative Scrapbooking

CHAPTER 4
Gift Scrapbooking

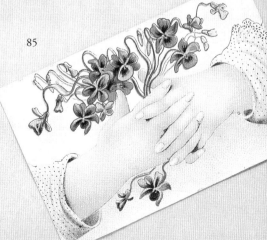

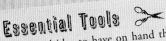

Essential Tools ✂

It's a good idea to have on hand the basic scrapbooking tools. However, we think it's also important to collect tools you love and will be able to keep using for a long time. Think carefully about what kinds of tools you'd like to have. When you find the perfect tool, add it to your collection.

Cutter knife

Cutter knives are used for cutting straight lines. They are also useful for complicated cutting jobs. Be sure to change blades periodically.

Scissors

For detailed cutting work, choose a type with pointed ends. Be sure to choose a pair of scissors that offer a snug fit.

Eyeleteer

This tool is designed to make eyelet holes, small holes which you can pass a cord lace, ribbon, pin, or button shank through.

Craft glue

Starch-based glue that can be applied with a paintbrush for projects involving larger pieces of paper.

Spray glue

This type of glue is perfect for those jobs where you want to work quickly. Because it is more expensive than other types of glue, it should only be used when you really need it.

Masking tape

Besides being used for decoration, masking tape will also serve as one of your main adhesive tools.

Pens/Pencils

The best utensils to write comments and messages are the types that are comfortable to use and that you are most used to using.

Tweezers

To be used for handling small parts, like beads, or to use to pick up paper during tea staining. This tool will help you work more quickly.

Cutting mat

The cutting mat should always be used when you use a cutter knife, so you don't damage the table where you are working. An 8" x 12" mat is a must.

Hole punch

This tool is similar to an eyeleteer, but is used to punch holes in paper. An eyeleteer designated as a paper eyeleteer will serve a similar purpose.

Paintbrush

These are useful for applying craft glue on large surfaces. Try and have a few different sizes available.

Glue stick

For gluing paper, the best glue to use is a stick glue. This type of glue is very versatile and will be one of your most useful tools.

Liquid glue

Liquid glue is used for plastic or wood and other non-paper items.

Stamps/Ink pad

Try and collect a variety of stamps, such as letters of the alphabet, numbers, or images you like. Then choose ink colors in your favorite shades.

Ruler

This is an essential tool, of course, for measuring; but it is also useful for cutting straight lines. Rulers that are transparent are especially useful.

Sewing kit

A sewing kit will come in handy for sewing buttons onto scraps, sewing on parts, or even for doing some embroidery. A needle and thread is enough.

A note about glue

In the "What you will need" section for each project, unless it says differently, a glue stick is what is being referred to for glue. Most of the projects in this book use a glue stick. Where there is a larger surface to cover, you can use a paintbrush to apply the craft glue.

Note: The other tools required for each project are indicated in "What you will need" section on the project's page.

Basic Techniques ✂

Here are five basic techniques that can be used in a wide variety of situations. Along with a big dose of creativity, mastering these things will help you on your way to scrapbooking success!

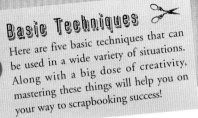

Cutting photos out to create silhouettes will give your scrapbook scenes a sense of movement.

1 *By carefully arranging your photos, you will make your scrapbooks more original*

Using photos of varying sizes will transform your design. You don't have to use special software for the photos; simple color copies of photos can work well. You can make copies leaving white margins to imitate the look of instant film prints, or cut photos into oval shapes or silhouettes. By cutting your photos into various shapes and making copies that simulate the look of different types of film, like color, sepia, or monochrome, you will add interest and variety to your scrapbooking layouts.

It is useful to keep small scraps of paper. Just staple them together or use an eyelet punch, until you are ready to use them.

2 *Creating image through paper*

A scrapbook's image is created by the kinds of paper that are used. For example, choosing flat, smooth white paper will evoke a sharper image. More textured papers will give warmth to your scrapbook page, while the transparent quality of tracing paper will create coolness. One of the most important kinds of paper is patterned paper, and it is a great idea to collect scraps of paper, such as pieces of cute wrapping paper or maps you bought on a trip somewhere. Paper with pictures can be cut out and used creatively as well.

3 Making full use of color copying

By making use of color copying, you can do all kinds of creative things. For example, by making a color copy of a piece of antique cloth, you will have a one-of-a-kind patterned background for a scrapbooking page. You can also make copies of things you want to keep, like maps or photos, that you don't want to cut up.

4 Tea, coffee, and wine staining

Why not try using tea, coffee, or wine to create an antique effect on paper or lace? By experimenting with ingredients and steep times, you can create a wide variety of shades.

Steep times will greatly affect color. The card on the left seeped for less than ten minutes, the card on the right seeped for more than thirty.

You can find old books to use for their beautiful pages at flea markets or from used bookshops.

5 Selecting materials from daily life

Things found at flea markets or stamp markets can be scrapbooking treasures. However, excellent materials can also be found as we go about our daily lives. Always be on the lookout for designs and images to cut out of magazines, collections of embroidery samples, and even things like cute baguette bags from the bakery. It is exciting to happen upon that "perfect item" as we go about our everyday lives.

CHAPTER 1

Easy Scrapbooking

The first five projects will present easy techniques for how to better use treasured photos, clippings from books and magazines that caught your fancy, colorful ribbon, and a variety of eye-catching motifs. Highly personal, scrapbooking is about using only the things you love in ways you love. Indeed, one of the greatest pleasures of this art form is getting inspired by an idea, but always giving the idea your own personal twist! By embracing creativity and your own personal style, you will enjoy scrapbooking even more.

This design incorporates the simple technique of cutting opens for inserting the edges of your photos on the page. It is easy to do, and by adding accents like old stamps or masking tape, or by gluing on decorative motifs, you can create sophisticated-looking pages.

WHAT YOU WILL NEED:

- *Photos*
- *Old stamps / Cutouts from old books / Label stickers / Bird-theme cutouts*
- *Memo labels*
- *Typewriter-theme masking tape*
- *8¹/₂" x 11" string-bound album (or ring-binder album)*
- *Cutter knife / Cutting mat / Glue / Stamps*
- *Pencil / Ruler*

1 Decide where you are going to attach the photo. Using a pencil, mark four spots ³/₈" from where the four corners will be. These marks will guide you when cutting the inserts for the photos. Glue on cutouts from old books before attaching the photos.

2 Using the pencil marks you made as a guide, cut inserts for the four corners of the photo. Because the insert cuts will be visible on the back of the pages, this scrapbook will only use the right side (or front side) of each page.

3 Make inserts for other photos. Then glue on labels with date stamps or comments, and accent with things like old stamps, bird-theme cutouts, or typewriter-theme masking tape.

After attaching the treasured photos to the pages, be sure to decorate the front of the book too. Give it a title, and you can decorate with a theme using accents like beads or cutouts.

PROJECT 2

Decorating with
Stickers and Maps

STICKERS ARE AN ESSENTIAL "MUST HAVE" FOR SCRAPBOOKS, AND REQUIRE NO TOOLS OR SKILLS TO USE THEM! MAPS ARE ALSO WONDERFUL BECAUSE THEY PUT EXPERIENCES IN PERSPECTIVE. WHEN YOU USE THEM CREATIVELY, THEY CAN TRANSFORM A PAGE INTO A NARRATIVE STORY.

WHAT YOU WILL NEED:

- *Photos*
- *Map / Thin paper*
- *Lace*
- *Frame corner stickers*
- *Stamp-theme stickers and label stickers*
- *12" x 12" or 8" x 8" spiral-bound album*
- *Glue / Liquid glue / Stamps*

1 First, decide where you will position your photo, then cut the map to an appropriate size and glue it beneath where the photo will be attached. Use your hands to tear out the map to give the layout a unique appearance.

2 Decorate the four corners of the photo with frame corner stickers. Using the frame stickers around the main photo will draw focus to the main point of interest on the page.

3 Use the stamps and label stickers to create titles, and add lace for further accents. If it feels appropriate, apply some stickers on an angle.

Stickers are fun to use on letters or cards, too. Using stickers on your envelopes or letters can make them look more elegant.

PROJECT 3
Using Masking Tape to Make Movies

ALL THAT IS NEEDED TO CREATE THIS INTERESTING OLD FILM EFFECT IS TO APPLY MASKING TAPE TO THE BORDERS OF YOUR PHOTOS. EACH PHOTO BECOMES "ONE SCENE" IN A UNIQUE FILM THAT YOU CREATE.

WHAT YOU WILL NEED:

• *Photos*
• *Cutouts from old magazines / label sheets*
• *Film-theme masking tape*
• *4" x 6" post-bound album*
• *Scissors / Stick glue / Stamp*

1 Apply film-theme masking tape to both the top and bottom border of each photo. Rather than ripping the tape off with your fingers, use scissors to cut each end of the tape at the corner to really give the feeling of old negatives.

2 Using the label sheets, stamp the date of each photo and attach. You can add accents with camera-theme masking tape or by using cutouts from old magazines.

USING MASKING TAPE TO FRAME PHOTOS WILL MAKE EACH ONE LOOK LIKE A PAINTING! THIS STYLE CONVEYS WARMTH AND WILL ALLOW YOUR MEMORIES TO INSPIRE WORKS OF ARTS.

WHAT YOU WILL NEED:

- *Photos*
- *Flower-theme accents or decorative items*
- *Ribbons / lace*
- *Frame-theme masking tape*
- *8" x 6" (or 8" x 8") post-bound album*
- *Scissors / stick glue / liquid glue*

1 Apply frame-theme masking tape to both the top and bottom border of each photo. Rather than ripping the tape off with your fingers, use scissors to cut the tape. Glue on the lace at the bottom of each photo before attaching the photos to the board.

2 Attach the masking tape to the sides of each photo to create a frame-like effect. By carefully cutting the edges of the tape at 45-degree angles, you will make it look more realistic. Use flower-theme accents or ribbons.

PROJECT 5

A Casual "Pinup"
Scrapbook

This scrapbook evokes the feeling of pinning your favorite pictures to the wall. By using brass pins, you can easily change the pictures later. Using label stickers to write comments or to create quote bubbles is also fun.

WHAT YOU WILL NEED:

- *Photos (Instant film is recommended)*
- *Old stamps / Cutouts from old books / Postcards / Labels*
- *Brass pins*
- *Quote bubble stickers*
- *Stripe and letter-theme masking tape*
- *6" x 8" (or 8¹/₂" x 11") post-bound album*
- *Eyeleteer / Cutting mat / Glue / Stamps*

1 Starting with the larger pieces, glue cutouts from old books or postcards into your album. Next, plan the layout of the photos and more detailed pieces in order to create a collage effect. The most important thing to keep in mind is balance in the layout.

2 Use stickers to write quote bubbles and comments. Then decorate with masking tape.

3 Push pins through each photo to secure it in place. (Make sure the cutting mat is beneath where you are working to avoid damaging the table.) Finally, add accents with stamps and label stickers.

Adding quote bubbles can add humor to photos and postcards. Points of interest highlighted on maps can also enhance your design.

CHAPTER 2

Travel Scrapbooking

Most people take many photos when they travel. However, travelers bring home more than just photos. When we travel, we also come home with keepsakes, like airline tickets and city maps, or even small things, like a sugar wrapper found in a café that you can't bring yourself to throw away. From the hustle and bustle of a town and the way it smells, to the people we meet on our trips—all of these things seem to engrave themselves in our memory. Evoking the many varied experiences of the trip, these are the kinds of precious memories we want to preserve forever in our scrapbook.

PARIS

Français

JOYEUSES PAQUES

CLICHY

SULFATE DE QUININ

Sacre Coeur

Palais Royal

Grds Boulevards

Tour Eiffel

FLEURS PECTORALES

Saint Germain

Cite

Lay down a map of Paris and then attach your favorite photos from the spots you loved there. Photos of the Eiffel Tower, the Palais-Royal, and the Sacré-Cœur will look attractive against a map of the city and accented with camera-themed decorative items. This scrapbook evokes a bird's-eye view of a beloved city, like Paris.

What you will need:

- *Photos*
- *Maps / Copy paper*
- *Cutouts from old magazines*
- *Plastic or metal number accessories / diorama figures*
- *Label stickers*
- *Brads*
- *12" x 12" (or 8½" x 11") spiral-bound album*
- *Cutter knife / Cutting mat / Eyeleteer / Paintbrush / Glue / Liquid glue / Stamps / Ruler*

1 Make a color copy of the city map and adjust the size so it will cover two side-by-side pages of the scrapbook when it is open. Then cut the copy down the middle to be used on the left page and the right page, and glue each side to the base of a page. If you can find an old map of the city, it will add charm to the layout.

2 Make small playing card–size color copy reductions of the photos. You can adjust the sizes depending on the map scale and the number of items you want to use in this scrapbook. Leave white margins on the copies so you can jot the place name for each photo.

3 Glue the photos to the map, then add brass camera accessories as accents. Be sure to glue the photos according to the place locations on the map. You could also add diorama figures or label stickers to add interest.

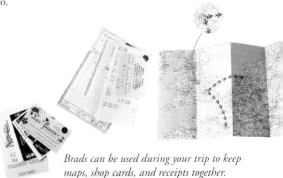

Brads can be used during your trip to keep maps, shop cards, and receipts together.

PROJECT 7

Beautiful Scenes
from the British
Countryside

The scenic beauty of the British countryside is captured in the style of an old movie in this scrapbook. This is the world of ivy-covered manor houses, streets lined with old brick buildings, and sheep grazing in the fields. Flipping through the pages of this scrapbook will make you feel like you are replaying the scenes from your trip.

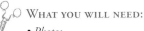

WHAT YOU WILL NEED:

- *Photos*
- *Cutouts from British newspapers / Old stamps*
- *Leaves*
- *Index stickers*
- *Camera-theme masking tape*
- *8" x 6" (or 8" x 8") spiral-bound album*
- *Cutter knife / Cutting mat / Glue / Stamps / Ruler*

1 Start by trimming the pictures. Cut them all to a uniform height (around 3" tall). There should be two or three per page to give the effect of looking at an old movie reel.

2 Glue the photos. Make sure not to leave any room between them. Below the photos, apply the film-theme masking tape, and then decorate with the camera-theme masking tape and label masking tape.

3 Add accents, such as cutouts from British newspapers or old stamps and leaves. Add the title in alphabet stamps, stamping each letter one by one. Then use index stamps to write Day 1, Day 2, etc.

Index labels are a great way to organize your book. Simply label the pages with dates and locations for easy reference. Afterward, you can easily flip to the day you are looking for!

PROJECT 8
A Scrapbook Journal
for Recording Special
Experiences

Mixing elements of a travel journal with a scrapbook, this book will help you capture the unique experiences from your trip. Photographs are essential. You could also use newspaper clippings from a particular day you were there or city maps to evoke what words alone couldn't—in order to create what will become a truly vivid record of your trip.

What you will need:

- *Photographs (Use instant film)*
- *Maps / Cut out clippings from foreign newspapers / Old stamps*
- *Letters and stationery-theme stickers*
- *Tag stickers*
- *Letter- and stationery-theme masking tape*
- *Small spiral-bound journal or datebook*
- *Glue / Stamps / Pens*

1 | If you're using a datebook, note events that happened on specific days of your trip. It's also fine to use a journal with no dates, because then you can start whenever you want and only write items for the days you want to describe.

2 | Use masking tape to attach photos from your trip. Instant film is useful since you can use it immediately while you are still traveling. Be sure to add comments next to each picture.

3 | Stamps and parts of maps or foreign newspapers also look nice. Add motif stickers or masking tape in the margins to add interest and color. Be sure to stamp the date on the tabs.

If you use too much ink, it can get all over the page and turn into a mess. To avoid this, carefully hold the ink pad in one hand and the stamp in the other, and then tap the stamp lightly against the ink pad several times before gently applying the stamp to your project.

Making use of treasured items found at garage sales or flea markets—like an old postcard of a cityscape from a hundred years ago, a children's book handed down for generations, or some fine, handmade lace from times past—will turn this scrapbook into a unique and precious treasure.

1 Cut the colored papers, patterned papers, and music sheets to the appropriate size for gluing onto the base. Using your fingers to gently tear out the paper will give a warmer, old-fashioned effect. You can also add lace.

2 Cut photos into oval shapes, then prepare strips of masking tape 2–3 times the length of each oval's circumference. Fold the edges of the tape back $^1/_{16}$-$^1/_8$ inches. If you need longer pieces, you can separate the tape into sections.

The washi (Japanese paper) masking tape is flexible and easy to use. With it, you can make a frill that has a hand-sewn, textured quality.

- *Photos*
- *Colored paper / Patterned paper / Music sheets / Lace paper / Glassine paper*
- *Old stamps / Postcards / Label sheets / Tags / Flower-theme accents*
- *Ribbon / Lace / Pearl beads / Butterfly accents*
- *Frame-theme masking tape*
- *8¹/₂" x 11" string-bound album (or ring-bound album)*
- *Cutter knife / Cutting mat / Scissors / Paintbrush / Glue / Liquid glue / Tweezers*

3 Glue on masking tape around the circumference of the oval-shaped photos. Gather the tape to create frills. After completing the entire circumference, finish off by decorating with ribbon, lace, or pearl beads.

4 Use glue to attach all elements and then add decorative items like three-dimensional butterflies. You can then create a collage using the old postcards, labels, and tags. Rather than thinking of separate pieces, aim to make each page a single work of art.

Collecting different kinds of masking tape is fun, but instead of sticking them in a drawer and forgetting they are there, try to use the tape in all kinds of creative ways. This requires organization. One great way to make efficient use of your tapes is to store them in such a way that you can quickly see what you have, such as by keeping them separated by style and color. You could even line them up in a small basket or buy a stacker. It is also a good idea to have a pouch or pencil case handy so you can grab your supplies when you're on the go!

Taking a stroll while on a holiday, you happen upon a merry-go-round. This fanciful image becomes the scene for a mini-scrapbook. By adding some horses or flower motif accents, you can create a scrapbook that is like an illustrated children's picture book. This petite work of art will become a treasured keepsake of your trip for you when you are back at home.

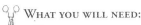

What you will need:

• *Photos*
• *Thick paper / Drawing paper / Copy paper*
• *Old stamps / Cutouts from old books / Label stickers / Horse-theme accessories and accents*
• *String*
• *Frame corner and label stickers*
• *Cutter knife / Cutting mat / Glue / Stamps / Ruler*

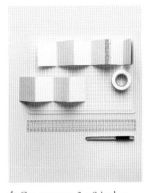

1 Cut paper to 3 x 9 inches and make a fold at every $2^{1}/_{4}$ inch. Make three of these folded sheets and attach each edge of them to the others to make one long accordion paper, so that you can make a 10-page book.

2 Make color copies of the photos, reducing the sizes so that they will fit within the pages of the book. Pictures should be approximately $2 \times 1^{1}/_{2}$ inches (and if they are horizontal $1^{1}/_{2} \times 2$ inches).

3 Trim cutouts, from things like old books, down to an appropriate size and glue them to the paper. Then glue the photos you prepared, and decorate with frame corner stickers and horse accents.

4 Cut a cover out of thick paper. The paper should be 3 inches tall and $4^{1}/_{2}$ inches wide. After you cut the paper, fold it in half. Fold up the book and then glue both ends to the interior sides of the cover. Use the label stickers to create a title. Finally, line the string around the middle of the book to shape it, and tie the two ends in a bow at the top.

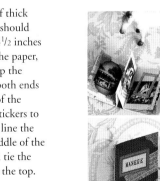

When you're in Paris, you always stop in an old-fashioned haberdashery. Like in a favorite café, you spend hours there lingering over the beautiful fabrics, laces, and buttons. Over the years, you have collected more than a few scraps from purchases there. Why not use a coffee stain to evoke the warmth of a delicious cup of café au lait you had around the corner from it? Be sure to also decorate the scrapbook with many ribbons and buttons that remind you of the shop.

What you will need:

- *Photos*
- *Drawing paper / Copy paper*
- *Cutouts from old books / Label stickers / Paper doilies / Sewing-theme accessories*
- *Ribbon / Lace / Buttons*
- *6" x 8" (or 8¹/₂" x 11") post-bound album*
- *Coffee / Bowl / Paper towels*
- *Cutter knife / Cutting mat / Glue / Stamps / Ruler / Tweezers*

1 Place three small pieces of drawing paper cut in the shape of business cards, but slightly larger, along with the paper doily in the coffee and let them sit for 5–10 minutes. Take them out and let them dry between two paper towels.

2 Make color copies of the photos, making them small enough to fit on the cards. Cut four photo inserts so that the four corners of the photos can be inserted, then attach the photos attached to the cards. The effect should look like matted photos.

3 Glue along the base of the cards to add labels and pieces of doilies. You can also add color copied sewing-theme images from magazines or books, and then decorate with things from the haberdashery, like lace and buttons.

White   Coffee   Tea

Wine

Along with drawing paper and paper doilies, you can also stain ribbons and lace. Coffee and tea will create an antique effect, while red wine will give a subdued pink stain. These stains will create unique, one-of-a-kind colors and help give a "homemade" feeling to your scrapbooks.

PROJECT 11
Inspiration from a Parisian Haberdashery

What to do with an antique card, old stamps, and a little bird button? Why not create a scrapbook where these precious small keepsakes from a past trip can be neatly lined up in the book as if stored away in a treasure box?

WHAT YOU WILL NEED:

- *Construction paper*
- *Old stamps / Cards / Label stickers / Decorations with a playful motif or theme*
- *Ribbons / Buttons / Accessories with a knit theme*
- *Frame-theme masking tape*
- *8" x 6" (or 8" x 8") post-bound album*
- *Cutter knife / Cutting mat / Paintbrush / Glue / Liquid glue / Ruler*

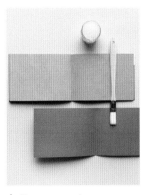

1 Cut construction paper to fit the album when it is laid open. Then, folding the paper in half, line up the center fold against the middle binding of the album and glue the paper to the base. Choose a color that will accent the souvenir items you will be using.

2 Use frame-theme masking tape around all four edges of the pages when opened. First do the top and bottom and then the two sides. Be sure to cut the tape at 45-degree angles, fitting the edges together for gluing.

3 Next, glue on the old stamps, cards, label stickers, and ribbons. Then, glue on the souvenir items as if lining them up on the bottom of a treasure box. Laying the items out carefully like pieces in an exhibition will make a strong impression.

For books that bulge because of the treasures, it is helpful to attach a ribbon or cord to be able to tie it shut when you aren't looking at it.

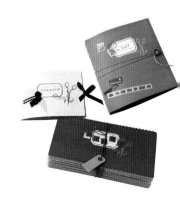

PROJECT 13
Revisiting a Favorite Romantic Inn

This scrapbook recreates in photos and small accessories a wonderful time spent in a small out-of-the-way inn. Like a dollhouse, items are set on small shelves, and the scene out the window is a German castle. This album aims to recreate the feeling of an unforgettable moment.

What you will need:

- *Photos*
- *Construction paper / Patterned paper*
- *Lace accents / Antique key accessories*
- *Small pieces of balsa wood (1/16–1/8 inch thick)*
- *Border stickers*
- *Frame-theme masking tape*
- *Miniature frames*
- *Miniature letters, packages, and books*
- *Label stickers*
- *12" x 12" (or 8 1/2" x 11") spiral-bound album*
- *Cutter knife / Cutting mat / Eyeleteer / Paintbrush (for glue) / Glue / Liquid glue / Stamps / Paintbrush (for paints) / Poster paints / Ruler*

1 Cut the construction paper and patterned paper to fit the album size and then glue them to the base. Next, use frame-theme masking tape to make borders.

2 Cut three pieces of balsa wood to 3/8 x 2 inches. Paint the wood pieces brown using poster paint. Let them dry completely. Touch up if there are uneven spots.

3 Glue the wood to the album. On top of the "shelves," decorate with mini-letters or books. Add border stickers to letters and books before gluing them on.

4 Cut photos to fit inside mini-frames. Glue photos and overlay with mini-frames. Add lace and label stickers.

PROJECT 14
A Challenging
Scrapbook Design Using
Scandinavian Fabric

norway

With exquisite fabric from Scandinavia, this scrapbook has a rich appearance. The warmth of the fabric's texture gives the photos a soft, elegant feeling. Using scraps from your favorite fabric will also embellish your scrapbook.

WHAT YOU WILL NEED:

- *Photos*
- *Cloth / White paper (washi paper or copy paper)*
- *Old stamps / Postcards / Label stickers*
- *Buttons*
- *8½" x 11" string-bound album (or ring-binder album)*
- *Board / Sponge / Brush (a hard, even-length bristle brush, like a shoe brush, is recommended)*
- *Cutter knife / Cutting mat / Paintbrush / Craft glue / Liquid glue / Stamps / Ruler*

1 Cut the fabric to a slightly all-around larger size than the album. On a flat board or worktable, spread the fabric with the pattern facing down. Take a damp sponge and smooth the wrinkles from the cloth.

2 Cut a piece of white paper to a slightly all-around larger size than the fabric. Mix water with the craft glue, then use a paintbrush to spread the glue on the paper, and then glue it to the fabric. Use the brush or your hands to again smooth out any wrinkles.

3 Using the brush, tap the entire surface of the paper to make sure the paper and fabric are securely glued together. Wait twenty-four hours for it to dry, then use a cutter knife to cut away the extra paper and take off the board.

4 Cut the piece down to the size of the album and glue it to the base. Then, glue on old stamps, postcards, and buttons, and arrange your pictures as you see fit.

Paris: the city where you always wanted to live; or Copenhagen: a city like in a fairytale. How about the city that inspired you: Amsterdam? Or the city of fantasies: Marrakech? Each city has its own unique charm and feeling, and experiencing these places in all their glory is the true pleasure of foreign travel. This scrapbook is a celebration of the act of traveling. By picking unforgettable views from a series of cities, you will make this scrapbook an inspiration to set out once again.

1 After designing the overall layout, cut each of the photos. Try to create a rhythmic design by varying the number of photos on a page. Some pages may have a single large photo while others have several smaller ones.

2 Glue patterned paper on some of the pages. Try and choose patterns that will complement the photos.

For Copenhagen photos, for example, a retro pattern paper may look pleasing, while Prague will look fantastic against a floral paper. The design of the scrapbook is a perfect way to convey the feeling and atmosphere of a place.

WHAT YOU WILL NEED:

- Photos
- Old stamps / Cutouts from old books / Label stickers / Alphabet motifs
- Antique key or other metal accessories
- Patterned papers

- Letter-theme masking tape
- Label plate
- Accordion-book album
- Cutter knife / Cutting mat / Eyeleteer / Paintbrush / Glue / Liquid glue / Stamps

3 Glue the photos and proceed from city to city. (Use only one city on a page.) In the margins, decorate each page with suitable old stamps and decorative accents and motifs.

4 Stamp the label stickers with the names of the towns. You can vary the shape or label color to create a more appealing design.

Label plates are good for scrapbooking, as well as covers of notebooks, journals and albums. Let's use colored or patterned paper for labels.

CHAPTER 3

Commemorative Scrapbooking

A special birthday or a Christmas spent with the whole family. The first time the baby laughed or the magnificence of the roses in full bloom in the garden. These special times stand out from our daily lives and are engraved in our memories. Commemorative scrapbooking is a way to give form to these memories—each one calling for a unique scrapbook of its own. To cherish special memories is an act of gratitude. It is also a treasure in itself.

A WONDERFUL BIRTHDAY PARTY IS THE THEME OF THIS SCRAPBOOK. USING MASKING TAPE FOR DECORATION, THE LIVELY FEELING OF THE DAY IS PERFECTLY CONVEYED IN THE BIRTHDAY CROWN AND DECORATIVE GARLAND. THE SCRAPBOOK ITSELF RECREATES THE CELEBRATION.

WHAT YOU WILL NEED:

- *Photos*
- *Drawing paper / Patterned paper*
- *Construction paper / Old stamps / Label stickers / Paper doilies*
- *Ribbon / Yarn / Crown accessories*
- *Typewriter-theme masking tape*
- *8¹/₂" x 11" spiral-bound album*
- *Scissors / Craft punch / Paintbrush / Liquid glue / Stamps*

1 Cut patterned paper to fit the scrapbook and glue it to the base. Cut construction paper to serve as a mat for the photos; it should be slightly larger than the photos. Glue the photos to the mats.

2 Cut 2-inch strips of masking tape and fold the strips over a piece of yarn. Fold strips over yarn at ¹/₅ inch intervals to create a decorated piece of string 8-inches long. Cut both sides of each strip to create triangle shapes. Make three decorated strings like this.

3 Glue the strings to the strips to make a draped banner effect around the photos. Decorate the area around the photos with ribbon and the crown accessories, and then add old stamps and write comments on label stickers. You can add further decoration using a craft punch.

You can dress up the people in the photos by gluing ribbon, lace, or tiny artificial flowers on or around them. This technique is also fun to use for handmade birthday cards.

SPRING

AUTUMN

A TYPICAL DAY AT HOME WITH THE
FAMILY—THIS TOO IS SOMETHING
CHERISHED. IN THIS SCRAPBOOK,
THE TREASURE OF OUR DAILY LIVES
IS CELEBRATED BY DOCUMENTING A
SIMPLE, AVERAGE DAY. HOW WOULD
YOU COMMEMORATE AN AVERAGE
DAY? HOW ABOUT IN A PHOTO
JOURNAL OF THAT DAY?

WHAT YOU WILL NEED:

- *Photos*
- *Label and silhouette stickers*
- *Patterned papers*
- *8" x 6" or 8" x 8" spiral-bound album*
- *Cutter knife / Cutting mat / Paintbrush / Glue / Stamps / Pencil / Ruler*

1 Cut the base paper to the appropriate size to cover the pages, then glue it to the album. Be sure to choose paper that will coordinate well with the photos. For example, here, the season is celebrated with the patterned paper. It recalls the color and feeling of spring.

2 After deciding the layout of the photos, use a pencil to mark the position of all four corners on the paper. The photo does not necessarily have to be positioned in the middle of the page. You could put it off-center, keeping in mind the label and decorative accents. Use the cutter knife to cut photo inserts for all four corners of the photo, and then slip the photo in.

3 Next, decorate with the stickers. Keep the balance of the page layout in mind and leave plenty of empty space on each page. Finally, add the title using stamps on the label stickers.

The use of stickers will create the overall impression and feeling of this album. Applying the stickers across the margins will allow the space to unfold, as in the photo to the left. Putting stickers directly on the photos, as in the photo to the right, enlivens it.

PROJECT 18
Using Tracing Paper to Paint Our Memories of Summer

A PHOTO TAKEN ON THE BEACH BECOMES A WORK OF ART WHEN FEATURED ON A WHITE CANVAS. THIS SUMMER SCRAPBOOK IS MADE USING COLOR COPIES ON TRACING PAPER AND THIN PIECES OF WRAPPING PAPER, ALONG WITH MASKING TAPE, TO CREATE A WISPY COLLAGE EFFECT AS COOLING AS A SUMMER BREEZE. THESE ARE THE HAPPY MEMORIES OF SUMMER.

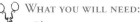

WHAT YOU WILL NEED:

- *Photos*
- *Canvas (small size)*
- *Patterned paper / Cutouts from old books / Wrapping paper / Tracing paper / Glassine paper*
- *Construction paper / Label stickers / Paper doilies*
- *Lace / Buttons / Artificial flowers / Three-dimensional cherry accessories*
- *Typewriter-theme masking tape*
- *Scissors / Craft punch / Paintbrush / Glue / Liquid glue / Tape*

1 Cut the base paper, patterned paper, cutouts from old books, and wrapping paper to suitable sizes and glue them onto the canvas. By creating a collage of overlapping paper, you will evoke a sense of transparency.

2 After gluing everything to the base, fold the paper to cover the edges of all four sides of the canvas and then cut off any extra paper protruding over the edges. Affix a long strip of masking tape along the entire outside edges of the canvas.

3 Make color copies of the photos on tracing paper and glue them to the base. Then decorate with three-dimensional accessories like cherries and artificial flowers, as well as masking tape. You can also add decoration using a craft punch.

Using just one piece of tracing paper, glassine paper, or wax paper will evoke a feeling of coolness and give more texture to any project, including cards and tags.

WOULDN'T IT BE FUN TO CAPTURE THE BEAUTY OF THE ROSES WHEN
THEY WERE IN THEIR FULL GLORY IN THE GARDEN? IF YOU HAVE THIS
MEMORY ON PAPER, YOU CAN KEEP IT WITH YOU ALL YEAR LONG AND
SHARE IT WITH YOUR FRIENDS.

1. Cut the patterned paper to fit the size of the scrapbook and then glue it to the base. Try to choose a pattern that will accentuate the theme of the roses, such as ivy or leaves.

2. Approximately $^5/_8$ inch from the bottom of the page, cut openings at $1^1/_5$ inches, $^3/_8$ inches, and $1^1/_5$ inches intervals. These holes are for threading the ribbon. The size of the holes should be appropriate for both the width and thickness of the ribbon.

To create a bold effect, we recommend using ribbon with texture, such as grogram or velvet. Scrap fabrics can also be used to create a more graphic design.

WHAT YOU WILL NEED:

- *Photos*
- *Patterned paper*
- *Ribbon / Small bird accessories*
- *Mini-frames*

- *8" x 6" or 8" x 8" post-bound album*
- *Cutter knife / Cutting mat / Paintbrush / Glue / Liquid glue / Tweezers*

3. Next, feed the ribbon through the holes. If it is difficult to feed the ribbon, you can use tweezers. After the ribbon is completely thread through all the holes, glue both ends down using liquid glue. You can also use the ribbon to make small bows.

4. Cut your photos so they fit inside the mini-frames. Glue the photos and then overlap the frames on top. You can use a variety of frame shapes as well as other items such as the birds to add interest.

Scraps are an essential part of crafting. They have a bad habit, however, of going missing just when you need them. Therefore, we recommend winding lace and ribbon scraps around colored pieces of board (keeping similar colors together). Buttons of all shapes and colors can be stored in glass jars. String can be wound around spools and stored in baskets. By being organized, you'll be able to make more creative and efficient use of your scraps.

For no other reason than you happened upon some delicious-looking desserts in a shop, you invite your friends over for a tea party. Creating an invitation like this will be the start of what is sure to become a truly lovely get-together. Your invitation will be beautiful like a tablecloth of lace, and will be a perfect keepsake for a future scrapbook of the party.

WHAT YOU WILL NEED:

• *Photos*
• *Music sheets / Paper doilies / Glassine paper / Flower accents / Spoon and sugar bowl accents*
• *Ribbon / Lace*
• *Patterned papers*
• *Scissors / Craft punch / Corner stickers / Glue / Stamps*

1 Use the craft punch to create decorative punches on all four corners of the square invitation. Making punches to create rounded corners will give a high-class feeling to the invitation.

2 Glue on the paper doily. Then glue the musical sheet and glassine paper on top to create a collage effect. Wrap a piece of lace and tie a ribbon around the photo with a bow. Next, glue the decorated photo on the paper.

3 Slip your message under the bow on the photo. Add flower accents and cutouts from magazines of tea party items like spoons and sugar bowls. Use the same decorations for the envelope.

Paper doilies or cute napkins are wonderful accents to use with photos of food—whether it be food from a tea party, a lunch in the park, or a fancy dinner.

PROJECT 21
A Rabbit in a Teacup!

mon ami

Is that a rabbit popping out of a teacup? This scrapbook is full of playful touches that make it perfect for displaying photos of children or a beloved family pet. By cutting the photos out into little silhouettes, the pages appear like those from the fantastic world of an illustrated children's book.

WHAT YOU WILL NEED:

- *Photos*
- *Cutouts from an old book / Postcards / Label stickers / Paper doilies / Wrapping paper / Teacup motifs*
- *Construction paper*
- *Memo labels*
- *8" x 6" or 8" x 8" spiral-bound album*
- *Cutter knife / Cutting mat / Scissors / Glue / Stamps*

1 Glue on the old book cutouts, postcards, and wrapping paper. Then, add the paper doily, flower decorations, and label stickers with words stamped on.

2 Make four copies of the photos and cut them out into silhouettes. Next, make a photocopy of an illustration of a teacup from a book and cut the copy into a silhouette. Then, make photocopies of the silhouette using four different color construction papers.

3 Arrange the silhouette photos inside the mouth of the teacups. You can arrange each a little differently; for example, in one, just have the ears popping out, while in another, the whole face. Glue them on.

Color doilies are a great scrap to use and can give a refined, artistic touch to your projects. They can be torn, cut, or used as is. They add charm no matter which way you use them.

PROJECT 22

A Mini Scrapbook–
Style Wedding Poster

A SCRAPBOOK-STYLE POSTER CAN BE CREATED USING A NOSTALGIC MONOCHROME PHOTO AND A TEA-STAINED PAPER DOILY. IT CAN BE USED AS A WELCOME POSTER FOR A PARTY AND THEN LATER AS A KEEPSAKE AT HOME.

WHAT YOU WILL NEED:

- *Photos*
- *Cutouts from an old book / Music sheets / Label / Paper doily*
- *Lace / Lace-motif accents / Pearl beads*
- *Artificial flower / Bird-theme motifs*
- *Mat board*
- *Tea bag / Bowl / Paper towels*
- *Scissors / Glue / Liquid glue / Stamps / Pen / Tweezers*

1 Stain the paper doily in a bowl of dark tea for 5–10 minutes. Remove when the color is suitably stained and then dry between paper towels.

2 Glue the stained doily, old book cutouts, and sheet music to the mat inside the frame-theme borders. Then, add a lace lining along the insides of the frames.

3 Make a black-and-white copy of the photo and cut to an appropriate size. Draw a heart on the photo and decorate with pearl beads.

4 Glue the photos, then stamp the title onto the label stickers. Finally, add lace or lace motif accents. You can also add bird accessories and the artificial flowers.

An old-fashioned round portrait of a baby is like a priceless heirloom. Let's use a frame of pure white lace around the precious baby's sweet chubby cheeks. This scrapbook can also be adapted for birth cards and gifts.

WHAT YOU WILL NEED:
• *Photos*
• *Patterned paper*
• *Ribbon / Lace / Buttons*
• *8^1/$_2$" x 11" spiral-bound album*
• *Needle and threads*
• *Cutter knife / Cutting mat / Scissors / Paintbrush / Glue / Liquid glue*

1 Cut the patterned paper to fit the scrapbook and glue it to the base. Cut the photo into a round shape centering around the baby's face and glue it to the middle of the paper.

2 Take the edge of the lace and sew gathers in approximately ^{1}/$_{16}$ -^{1}/$_8$ inch intervals to create a ruffled effect. Make it long enough to fit around the circumference of the photo.

3 Glue the lace around the photo, and glue the full piece to the front cover of the album. If you want to create a fuller effect, you can make another lace border and glue them together. You can also add ribbon and white buttons.

Adding ribbons can add a lovely effect to your scrapbooks. There are so many types to choose from; they come in fabrics such as moleskin or satin, and have loads of different patterns. When using ribbon to make bows, only glue the back of the bow's knot to the paper. This will preserve the three-dimensional effect.

From birth to baby's first steps and baby's first words to becoming a sweet young lady, this scrapbook traces the life of your little girl. The color of red wine dyes the lace doilies to the perfect shade of pale pink, so reminiscent of girlhood.

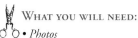

WHAT YOU WILL NEED:

- *Photos*
- *Patterned paper*
- *Cutouts from old books / Labels / Paper doilies / Flower motifs*
- *Ribbon / Lace / Flower accessories / Pressed flowers*
- *Patterned paper*
- *Memo labels*
- *Label stickers*

- *Frame-theme masking tape*
- *Accordion-style album*
- *Red wine / Bowl / Paper towels*
- *Cutter knife / Cutting mat / Scissors / Paintbrush / Glue / Liquid glue / Stamps / Tweezers*

1 Glue different types of patterned paper to each of the pages. Leave a space at the bottom as a margin to write the titles. Working page to page, the book should create a rhythm and story.

2 On each page, glue a photo and then add frame-theme masking tape to frame each picture. Start with the top and bottom frames. Then cut the tape at 45-degree angles and carefully attach it to the left and right sides.

3 Place the paper doily in the bowl of red wine for 5–10 minutes. When it is stained to the color you like, remove the doily and dry it between paper towels.

4 On each page, attach labels with the year stamped on them. Decorate with the wine-stained doily, flower accents, ribbon, and lace.

WHAT LIES HIDDEN BEHIND THOSE MITTENS? OPENING THE "MITTEN DOORS,"
WE FIND A CHRISTMAS TREE AND A FAVORITE PHOTO. IT IS AS IF THE MITTENS ARE
LOVINGLY HOLDING THE PHOTO. CELEBRATING THE JOY OF THAT ONE DAY OUT OF
THE YEAR, THIS SCRAPBOOK WILL SURELY DRAW A SMILE.

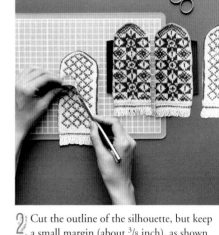

1. Make a color copy of the tops and bottoms of a favorite pair of mittens (four copies total). Reduce the copy size to fit your scrapbook. Glue the copies of the mitten bottoms onto the color construction paper.

For a Christmas theme, be sure to use lots of green and red, as well as Christmas tree motifs.

2. Cut the outline of the silhouette, but keep a small margin (about $3/8$ inch), as shown in the above photo, for the copies of the top mittens. This is where the glue will be applied. On the bottom mittens, cut along where the thumbs are of each side to create openings so that the photo can be placed.

WHAT YOU WILL NEED:

- *Photo*
- *Mittens / Copy paper*
- *Drawing paper / Construction paper / Patterned paper / Old stamps / Postcards*
- *Santa Claus and Christmas tree motif decorations*

- *Yarn / Felt / Rhinestones*
- *8¹/₂" x 11" string bound (or spiral -bound) album*
- *Cutter knife / Cutting mat / Scissors / Craft punch / Glue / Liquid glue / Stamps / Tweezers*

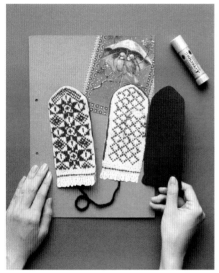

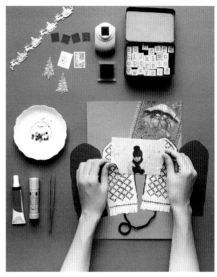

3 | Glue on accents like postcards and then glue on the two bottom gloves. Be sure not to get glue on the cutouts by the thumbs of the bottom gloves. Attach the glued margin of the top gloves underneath the black copies to create a door effect. Then put a piece of yarn to connect the gloves at the base.

4 | Place the photo in the thumb inserts; then, add tree motif accents and felt or rhinestones to decorate. You can decorate the margins by creating accents with the craft punch and then by decorating with a stamped message.

Commemorative scrapbooks can be made as gifts for birthdays or holidays. If you wrap the scrapbooks up in original, handmade wrapping, it will be even more special. By adding a small corsage or a cute card and wrapping it up using Tyrolean ribbons, instead of ordinary string, it will make a lasting impression.

CHAPTER 4

Gift Scrapbooking

A scrapbook of treasures created for someone special is truly a gift from the heart. A gift that is lovingly handmade with a particular person in mind is perhaps one of the most touching gifts one can receive. Maybe there will be handmade gift tags or a card that can be displayed to decorate an interior; these will preserve a meaningful message. With a little creativity and time, you will truly move a dear friend or loved one.

PROJECT 26
A Gift Tag that Can Be Used as a Bookmark

When wrapping up a gift for a friend, how about creating a gift tag that can be a bookmark? In addition to the gift itself, a tag can also be a great keepsake.

 What you will need:

- *Photos*
- *Old stamps / Paper doilies / Bird accents*
- *Ribbon / Lace / Leaves / Grommets*
- *Brads / Corner stickers*
- *Typewriter-theme masking tape*
- *Postcards*
- *Cutter knife / Cutting mat / Hole puncher / Glue / Liquid glue / Stamps / Ruler*

1 Make a sepia print of the photo and cut it to fit the size of the card. Glue the photo on the card, along with a paper doily. You may glue the photo on an angle.

2 Put corner stickers on all four corners of the photo and decorate with bird accents, brads, and masking tape. Use stamps to create a message, and then punch a hole and tie a piece of ribbon.

PROJECT 27
Sharing Memories of a Special Day

How about creating photo bags for your friends to put the prints you made from that special day? All you need is a transparent envelope and some decorations to create a wondrous container.

WHAT YOU WILL NEED:

- *Photos*
- *Cutouts from old magazines / Small card / Tags / Mini-envelope*
- *Brads*
- *Camera-theme masking tape*
- *Small paper bags for photos*
- *Hole puncher / Craft punch / Stamps*

1. Use the craft punch to cut either side of the top corner of the paper bag. Stamp the date on the label-theme masking tape and attach it to the corner of the bag. Decorate using the camera-theme masking tape.

2. Put the photos inside the paper bag and affix tags decorated with stamps and a mini-envelope containing a small card. Punch a hole through the envelope and tags and attach them with a brad.

PROJECT 28
Scrapbook-Style
Cards from a Group
of Friends

For special occasions, like when you want to cheer on a dear friend embarking on a new life adventure or celebrate a special milestone, it's meaningful to have your group of friends give that person scrapbook-style cards. Using mini-envelopes, you can create tiny messages that will be treasured by the recipient. Each letter will be for the eyes of the recipient only.

WHAT YOU WILL NEED:
- *Construction paper / Patterned paper / Copy paper*
- *Old stamps, / Cutouts from old books / Postcards*
- *Ribbons / Lace motifs / Buttons / Flower accessories*
- *Patterned papers*
- *Card stock and envelope set*
- *Cutter knife / Cutting mat / Craft punch / Glue / Liquid glue / Ruler*

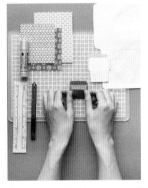

1. Make a reduced-size copy of an opened envelope. Using this as a template, make mini-envelopes in various sizes using color construction paper and patterned paper.

2. Glue cutouts from old books and postcards on a piece of card stock. Then wrap the card with the ribbon in a cross. If you use two types of ribbons and overlap them, it will give volume to the card.

3. Write your messages on tiny pieces of paper, place them in the envelopes, and glue the envelopes on the card with their openings facing up. You can enhance the card with bits of lace or flower accessories and then finish by adding more decorative elements using the craft punch.

Be sure to coordinate the look of the gift card with the paper and envelopes for an elegant touch!

This is a one-of-a-kind gift created from your photographs. Just make photocopies of the pictures, cut them into different sizes, decorate them, put them in a pretty box, and voila! You have just made a wonderful present.

WHAT YOU WILL NEED:

- *Photos*
- *Construction paper / Box*
- *Cutouts from old magazines / Wax paper, glassine paper, or other types of thin paper*
- *Lace / String / Metal accessories / Eyeleteer*
- *Stamp, label, and tag stickers*
- *Typewriter- and letter-theme masking tape*
- *Paper bag*
- *Mini-paper bag*
- *Cutter knife / Cutting mat / Scissors / Hole puncher*
- *Craft punch (border patterns) / Glue / Liquid glue / Stamps*

1 Make color copies of photos on construction paper cut to a postcard size. Cut and leave margins, then decorate with stickers and masking tape.

2 Make color copies of photos on construction paper. Cut the paper to the size of a business card, then decorate with the craft punch and masking tape.

3 Make color copies of photos on construction paper, then cut the paper into tag shapes ($2^{1}/_5$ x $1^{1}/_5$ inches). Decorate with masking tape. Use a grommet to make a hole, then put a string through it and tie.

4 Put the tags and mini-cards into the mini-bags, then put them all in the box. Decorate the box with cutouts from old magazines and thin paper such as wax or glassine paper.

PROJECT 30
A Garland to Adorn an Interior Space

An unforgettable way to say thank-you to someone, this garland is made from special photos, an antique card, and flower decorations. Made up of only five letters to form the word "merci," it is something that will give pleasure from the moment it is taken out of the envelope. It will be destined to later become part of the room décor of its recipient.

1 Cut thick paper into circles with a 3 $^{11}/_{16}$-inch circumference. Or, if you prefer, gather circle-shaped coasters.

2 Next, glue on photos, cutouts from old books, labels, construction paper, patterned paper, old stamps, postcards, flower decorations and masking tape. Finally, add the letters. You can use a stamp or cut letters out from a magazine.

This garland is a perfect decoration for a room—maybe in the window or perhaps on the wall. Try and choose accents and paper colors that will go well with the recipient's home.

WHAT YOU WILL NEED:

- *Photos*
- *Thick paper*
- *Construction paper / Patterned paper / Old stamps / Cutouts from old books*
- *Postcards / Label / Alphabet-theme accents / Flower decorations*
- *Ribbon*
- *Frame-theme stickers / Letter- and stationery-theme stickers*
- *Letter-theme masking tape*
- *Small envelope*
- *Scissors / Glue / Liquid glue*

3 Line up your message and then glue the ribbon on the backs to connect the circles. Make sure it stays perfectly straight so none of the letters is tilting to an angle. To hang nicely, keep about a ⁴/₅ inch space between each circle.

4 Pile the cutouts or coasters on top of each other like an accordion, and then put them inside a small envelope. For a perfect presentation, place the end ribbon at the opening of the envelope.

To go with this special present, how about creating a card to match? You can use three-dimensional decorative items, like an antique key, on the card to give it more impact.

Creator's Profile

Aya Nagaoka

As an editor and craft planner, Aya Nagaoka creates scrapbooking and collages accented by antique European paper goods such as antique cards, vintage stamps, and scrap pictures. She is the author of numerous books such as *Sukurappuhorikku no Hon* ("The Scrapaholic's Book"), *Masukingu Tepu de Koraju* ("Making Collages by Masking Tape"), and *Furenchi Koraju Ressun* ("French Collage Lesson").

MOTIF
COLLECTION
Useful Illustrations and Patterns

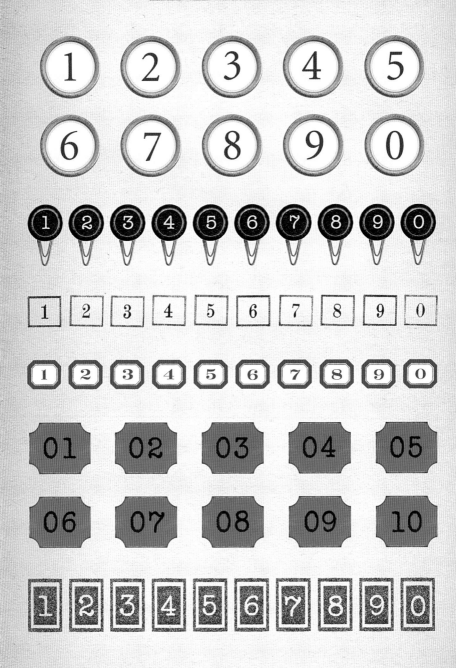

MESSAGES

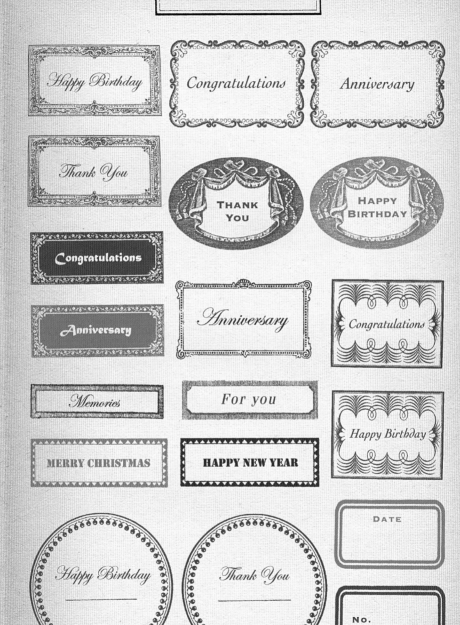

Happy Birthday

Congratulations

Anniversary

Thank You

THANK YOU

HAPPY BIRTHDAY

Congratulations

Anniversary

Anniversary

Congratulations

Memories

For you

Happy Birthday

MERRY CHRISTMAS

HAPPY NEW YEAR

Happy Birthday

Thank You

DATE

NO.

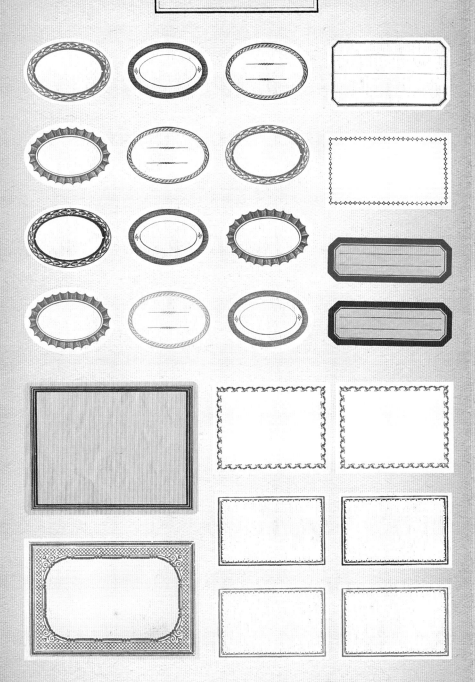

LABELS

STAMPS

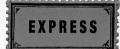

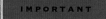
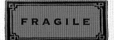

TAGS

Nº————
————
————

ADDRESS
————
————

ADDRESS
————
————

ADDRESS
————
————

ADDRESS
————

12 | 11 | 10 | 9 | 8 | 7

1 | 2 | 3 | 4 | 5 | 6

OPEN HERE

OPEN HERE

OPEN HERE

OPEN HERE

OPEN HERE

OPEN HERE

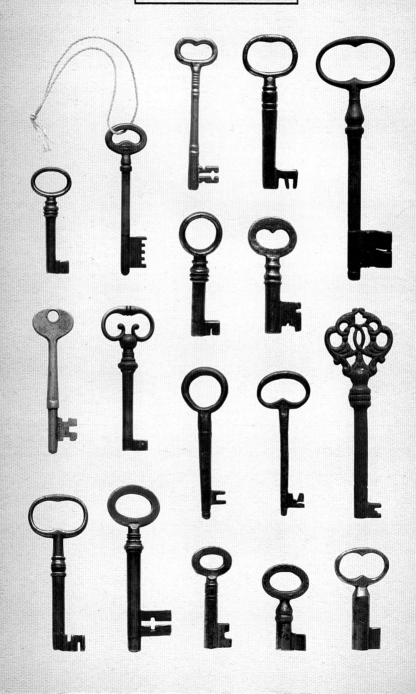

STATIONERY

SEWING

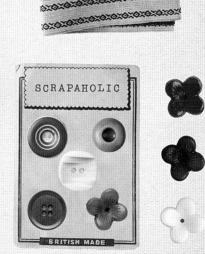

FLOWERS